J.

S

The Colour of
ONTARIO

Largest of provinces in population, resource-rich Ontario sits smack in the middle of Canada, the heartland of the nation with a land area of 412,582 square miles, which extends from the cold arctic tundra of Hudson Bay to the deciduous forest of Point Pelee. Ontario is bigger than Germany, France, and the United Kingdom combined. If you travel the Trans-Canada Highway at the speed limit, without stopping to marvel at the beautiful scenery, it will take you three days to drive completely across the province. Most people take longer.

Home to more than eight million people, most of whom live in the southern part of the province one hundred miles from the United States border, Ontario has a racially varied population that is growing every year.

Broker to the nation, head office of the country, connected to the oceans of the world by both the Saint Lawrence Seaway and Hudson Bay, Ontario exports manufactured goods, raw materials, and her expertise.

Travelling about by car, canoe, airplane, and on foot I explored my home province. I poked into small towns, big cities, wilderness lakes, back roads, and isolated northern settlements. I talked to the people and took photographs. I liked what I heard and saw of Ontario, and I hope you will too.

The Frontier

Northern Ontario includes the land north of the line running from Rainy River in the west, through North Bay to the Quebec border in the east. It is a vast, largely unpopulated region of swamp, rock, primeval forest, mosquitoes, and blackflies. The inhabitants of this wilderness cluster around its mines and paper mills, or cling precariously to the right-of-ways of its few highways and railroad lines.

There is wealth in the form of minerals and timber hidden in this vast land, but it requires guts, determination, and luck, to wrestle it out. Most people come to the frontier to stake their claim, blaze a trail, make a buck, and then leave. Some of these pioneers decide that they like it here and they stay permanently. But for every one that stays, at least ten leave for more southern climes.

Many southerners reminisce at length about the years of their lives they worked in the gold mine at Timmins, manned the firetower near Atikokan, taught school in Moosonee, cut pulpwood at Iroquois Falls, or ran a paper machine at the mill at Kenora. They came north but they did not remain. The north is not the easiest place in which to live.

Kenora's waterfront with all the elements that constitute the wilderness of Northern Ontario.
First there are the bush pilots, that special breed of men who daily pit their flying skill against wind and weather. Their task is to ferry geologists, miners, hunters, and fishermen to lonely remote spots on the vast chunk of rock, lakes, and trees called the Canadian Shield.
Then there are the loggers, whose handiwork floats in huge timber rafts destined for the pulp and paper mill across the bay. They come into town from time to time to relax and spend some — or all — of their hard-gotten gains. Finally there are the remnants of the native people. They have been cut adrift from the moorings of their own culture; at the same time they have been denied the right to — or have been unwilling to — adopt the alien culture of the intruding white man.
Northern Ontario is a vast unpopulated wilderness, and frontier towns like Kenora are its lifeline.

Poised on the edge of the wilderness, Kenora's waterfront is the gateway to North Western Ontario. A water-based air force will whisk you into the wilds.

Highway No. 17, the southern branch of the Trans-Canada Highway, pierces the primeval forest in Lake Superior Provincial Park.

A sign at one gasoline station warns the motorist of no gasoline for the next 52 miles, until he reaches the town of Wawa. Wrestled from the wilderness and blasted through the hardest rock in the world, the highway bobs and weaves like a prize-fighter, around a piece of bottomless muskeg here or over a piece of unyielding rock there. Straight stretches, such as this one near Agawa Bay, result in a flurry of passing cars, or in a short burst of speed to be followed by slower driving enforced by the curving, undulating roadway. Most travellers rush headlong towards the grain fields of the west or the cities of the east encased in their cars like astronauts in a spacecraft. Stop your car and step a hundred yards into the misty forests and you step back a thousand years into the land of the Ojibway tribe and the great spirit Manitou. To a land that had never seen a white man, where travel was by canoe, not by car, and distance was measured by moons, not by miles.

Left: St. Thomas Anglican Church, Moose Factory

Right: The Dome Mine, Timmins

It is ironic that the window of St. Thomas Anglican Church on Moose Factory Island should take the same shape as the headframe of the Dome Gold Mine near Timmins. Both men of the cloth seeking human souls and the men of commerce seeking material riches are inextricably bound up together in the northern mystique. In the early days, missionaries not only saved the Indian's soul but also convinced him of the value of materialism necessary to support a trading economy.

Today the pendulum is starting to swing the other way, and the church is being changed by that very culture that it had tried to change so many years ago. In St. Thomas Anglican Church the altar cloth is of beautiful beaded moosehide, and the hymn books and service appear in the language of the Cree nation.

On the commercial side, the ladies' auxiliary runs a snack bar and gift shop in the church hall for tourists who wander in from the Polar Bear Express. Here delighted shoppers can find something to eat, can rest, and can buy beautiful necklaces and beadwork at fair prices from friendly Cree grandmothers.

The Dome Gold Mine near Timmins is one of the oldest mines in the region. It resulted from a discovery by Harry Preston in 1909 of a vein of quartz that contained so much gold that it was nicknamed "The Golden Sidewalk."

Black bears range over all of the forested areas of northern Ontario and usually do not bother humans except in instances where the bears have grown accustomed to man through begging food, or where an unsuspecting walker comes between a mother and her cubs.

Bears are quite often encountered in the evening, beside roadways. Under no circumstances should they ever be offered food, even from the relative safety of a car. Bears that have been fed lose their fear of man and become dangerous. They will eat just about anything and might decide, after dining on the bread crusts you so kindly offered, to eat the rest of your lunch, or your fingers, or your feet, or your head, for dessert.

My father likes to tell the story about a boyhood raspberry-picking expedition in which he and a bear ended up picking from opposite sides of the same bush. It seems that he and the bear, upon discovering each other, locked eyes for a few seconds and then both ran off in opposite directions as fast as their legs would carry them.

Left: Black Bear
Ursus americanus

Right: Moose/Alces alces

Common Loon/Gavia immer

The Moose has given its name to such places as Moose Factory, Moosonee, Moose River Crossing, Moose River, and two Moose Lakes. It seems that the front of every gas station, restaurant, motel, wilderness outfitters, or establishment catering to the tourist or hunter is adorned with a great plastic or plaster replica of a moose, all done up with varying degrees of good taste and artistic skill.

The loon has disappeared from most of its former range in the southern part of the province. But in northern Ontario, unlike the moose, it is still frequently seen, with one mating pair for each lake being the average number.
The cry of the loon has been described by some as blood-curdling, but I think of it as haunting. In any case, no one has truly experienced northern Ontario without hearing the cry of a loon piercing the deafening early morning silence of a mist-shrouded lake.

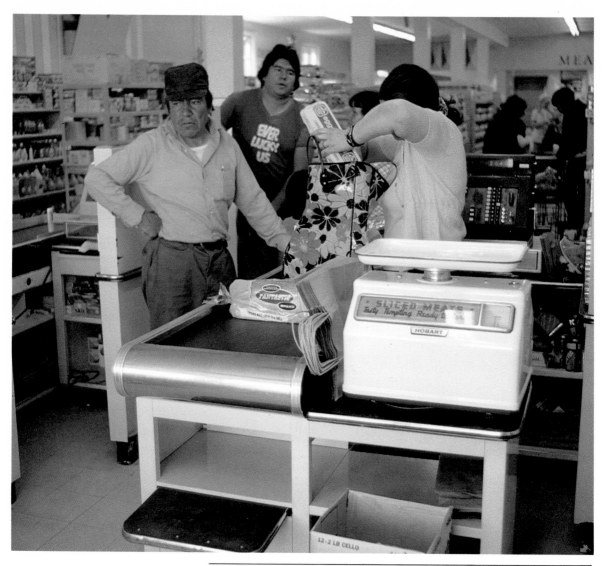

Left: Hudson Bay Company Post, Moose Factory Island

Right: Nickel smelter at Copper Cliff

The north is changing, and nowhere is this change better illustrated than in the Hudson's Bay Company store on Moose Factory Island. The post, the second-oldest post of the company, was originally established in 1673. In those days, trader and Indian bartered furs for rifles across a counter done up with iron bars like an old-time bank teller's cage. Selection was limited, and stock could only be delivered to the isolated post during the summer months when the supply ship from England would brave the Arctic waters of Hudson Bay. The completion of the Ontario Northland Railway in 1932 to the nearby town of Moosonee ended the isolation. The bars over the counter are down now, the medium of exchange is cash, and the customers push their shopping carts around in a modern, self-serve supermarket and department store identical to those in the far-away south. They also have to contend with the inevitable lineup at the check-out counter.

A northern problem, much more serious than the check-out counter, is the ecological damage left behind by some forms of industrial development. The nickel mines at Sudbury have so devastated the landscape that the traveller thinks he has landed on the moon.

The problem in Sudbury has been that air pollution from the smelter first kills the vegetation, and after prolonged exposure kills the workers. The solution has been to build the world's tallest chimney, thereby spreading the pollution over a greater area.

Residents of these northern towns are realistic enough to realize that they have to work somewhere, and without the polluters the towns would not exist. They have relied on their elected representatives to maintain a delicate balance between ecological considerations and employment opportunities. The evidence of the politicians' success as impartial referees in this life-and-death struggle is seen in the above photograph, taken just outside Sudbury.

Left: Husky dog-team

Right: Sunset Agawa Bay, Lake Superior

The snowmobile has had the same effect on the ground that the aircraft has had in the air, and that the kicker (or outboard motor, as it is known in the south) has had on the water. It has opened up vast areas of the country to the casual traveller. It has simplified the job of running a trap line, of staking a claim, of surveying a township, or of moving the sick and injured to a rail line.

Today, teams of husky dogs are kept only by northerners interested in racing them for sport. Snowmobiles may be more efficient, but no one can keep warm on the trail overnight by snuggling up to a machine. Nor can one eat a carburetor in an emergency.

There is nothing romantic about straining mile after uphill mile to help an exhausted dog team pull a fully loaded sled, or about spending the long dark cold winter in a log cabin barely big enough for a single bed. Most of the changes in the north are for the better and northerners welcome them. There are some things about the north that will never change, however, and the sight of the sun setting over Lake Superior is one of them.

The Breadbasket

Southwestern Ontario covers that area between Lake Huron and Lake Erie south and west of the Niagara Escarpment. Although cities such as London and Windsor are industrialized, the area is primarily one of large and highly productive farms.

Its location between the two Great Lakes moderates the climate considerably, so that winters are the warmest in the province. The area has often been referred to as the Banana Belt. It is too cold for such tropical crops as bananas, of course, but a sub-tropical crop like tobacco flourishes here.

With the exception of the lush green growth, due to the high rainfall, much of this flat, mostly treeless agricultural area resembles the prairie area of Manitoba and Saskatchewan. Here are huge fields of wheat harvested by giant combines, and straight flat roads that arrow their way towards a distant horizon capped by an immense sky. In the west part of southern Ontario, farmers in pickup trucks and cowboy hats ride the range.

This grassland similiarity to the Prairies has also been recognized by such prairie animals as the badger, coyote, turkey vulture, and gray partridge which have moved into the area from the Canadian west.

The skyscrapers dominating the end of Ouellette Street in Windsor are not part of Windsor or Canada at all. They are, in fact, across the river in Windsor's sister city of Detroit. The International Boundary Line is somewhere out in the river between those skyscrapers and the end of Ouellette Street, but to the casual observer on either shore the existence of any real barrier to any sort of movement and communication is almost impossible to detect.

It is only a few minutes between the two countries by either bridge or tunnel, and residents commute internationally to jobs, shopping, or nights out on the town. The automobile industry dominates the area, and the international nature of the business, confirmed in Canadian-United States treaties, has drawn the two cities even closer together.

In the first week of July, Windsor throws a big bash called the Freedom Festival that celebrates not only Canada's Dominion Day but also the American Independence Day. About the only thing the two cities do not have in common is that Windsor has been spared Detroit's high crime rate.

Ontario has always been close to the United States, but it is most obvious looking down Windsor's Ouellette Street. The cars are in Windsor, the skyscrapers are in Detroit.

Left: Tobacco field near Delhi

Right: University of Western Ontario, London

Stratford Festival Playhouse, Stratford

Tobacco, a crop of more southerly climes, grows near Delhi. The area along the Lake Erie shore has been referred to as "The Sun Parlour," and the truth is that winters are un-Canadian in their mildness, due to the moderating influence of the Great Lakes and a latitude as southerly as that of northern California. While tobacco may surprise visitors expecting northern pines, it raises a different emotion in those who earned their university tuition by stooping and bending in the back-breaking harvest.

Not everyone who attends the University of Western Ontario needs to earn his or her summer earnings picking the tobacco leaf. But if one has to it is worth going through the hardship of the tobacco fields just to be able to attend. Its school of Business is world-famous and has graduated many of our captains of industry. Situated on the outskirts of the medium-sized city of London, the beautiful campus is so large that students usually commute between classes by means of bus, car, or bicycle.

Stratford was, like London, named after an English city. To complete the English connection, Stratford is the home of the world-renowned Stratford Festival. Shakespeare's plays are presented every summer in a specially constructed theatre located in a park near the banks of the Avon River. Theatre buffs come from all over North America to attend. What better place, then, for a group of schoolboys to play a game like soccer than on the common in front of the Festival Theatre.

JAMOES~B
PORT DOVER

Port Dover is a small picturesque town with excellent beaches and a large summer population. I remember it, in the days of my youth, as a place that had one of the most popular dancehalls on the North Shore. The dancehall is still there and still popular with the younger crowd. But if the place hasn't changed, then I have. On a recent visit I was less intrigued by the dancehall than I was by the fact that Port Dover is the home of the Lake Erie commercial fishing fleet.

The docks are stretched out along the banks of the river that provides access to Lake Erie. Here trucks from Toronto, Hamilton, and Windsor load up at the fish wholesaler. Fishermen repair their nets and hang them up to dry. The turtle-shaped fishing boats come and go. A fisheries inspector takes off his official hat and spends a moment in pleasant conversation with an old friend. And carried in the breeze is the smell of fresh-caught fish.

With a little imagination, you could be in a far-away Atlantic or Pacific fishing village, and not smack in the middle of the continent in deepest Ontario.

The Golden Horseshoe

Rimming the western end of Lake Ontario, from Niagara-on-the-Lake around past Hamilton and Toronto to Oshawa, is a strip of highly industrialized land that contains a large proportion of the population of the province.

Oshawa, Brampton, and Oakville manufacture automobiles. Toronto is the cultural, administrative, and light-manufacturing centre of the province, while heavy industry is grouped around the steel mills at Hamilton. The only remaining productive farmland in the area is the fruit belt of the Niagara Peninsula. This is only temporary, however, as factories are now creeping out over the orchards and vineyards.

The Golden Horseshoe is where it's at. Life moves to the tune of the factory whistle and the roar of the expressway. Young men and women flock here to establish fast-paced, hectic careers. To some it is an invigorating atmosphere and they thrive on it. Others, less fortunate, cannot stand the pace and the Horseshoe hits them with ulcers, heart-attacks, and nervous breakdowns.

Planners are predicting that the Golden Horseshoe will some day be one giant city. The evidence is here already, as new subdivisions and factories quickly fill up the fast-disappearing open spaces between cities and towns.

The Toronto Island Ferry provides a cool breezy refuge from Toronto's summer heat, and an excellent view of the constantly changing skyline of Ontario's largest city.

The Toronto Islands are only a pleasant ferry ride from downtown Toronto and one of the best spots to view the latest additions to the city's constantly changing skyline.

The ferry ride itself is straight out of one of Stephen Leacock's stories, with kids riding on bikes, mothers chasing children off the upper railings, teenagers holding hands, sportily dressed men-about-town bound for one of the Island's yacht clubs, young women bursting out of shorts two sizes too small, all being presided over by a captain dressed in his blue uniform with gold braid and wearing a huge shaggy beard that looks as if he had just walked out of an advertisement for Jamaican rum.

The tallest free-standing structure in the world, the CN Tower, dominates the skyline. It does not matter where you are in the city, just look up and there it is, looming overhead. Torontonians have called it everything from a waste of money to names too rude to print here. They should be reminded, however, that Parisians initially said similiar things about the Eiffel Tower.

Above: Ontario Place

Right: New City Hall

Created on man-made islands opposite the Canadian National Exhibition grounds, Ontario Place celebrates all the things that are good about living in Ontario. The amusement complex boasts of a marina, restaurants, movies shown on the circular dome of the Cinesphere, and local and international performers appearing at The Forum.

Nathan Philips Square, in front of the new Toronto City Hall, is the heart of the city. There is a sense of excitement about the place, as lawyers on their way to the nearby courthouses mingle with Bay Street office workers, shoppers from Eaton's and Simpsons, residents of the nearby Chinese community, and school children on a City Hall tour.

Public meetings are held in the square, city politicians come and go, and television newsmen may even ask you for an opinion on one of the issues of the day. Even in the coldest days of winter, skaters glide across the rink in time to recorded music.

In the early 1950's, Toronto was a dull conservative city. The places to go for a little weekend fun were Montreal, Buffalo, or Detroit. Now the traffic has reversed, and weekends in Toronto are sold by the hotelful to the citizens of these American cities. Montrealers have not yet succumbed to our charms, but they do not compare the two cities the way they used to.

The catalyst in this change from staid provincial capital to cosmopolitan city was a revolution in Hungary in 1957. The Hungarian refugees were people who, once they got on their feet financially, patronized the theatres, restaurants, art galleries, and could not understand what was sinful about drinking wine with a meal on Sunday. Instead of disappearing into a small tight community, as other ethnic groups had done before them, they introduced Torontonians to their way of thinking.

They opened coffee shops on Yorkville Avenue and they went to court to win the right to wear bathing suits in city parks. Suddenly Toronto discovered that it had not only a Hungarian population but also Jews, Italians, Chinese, Lithuanians, Germans, Japanese, Portuguese, West Indian, and any other group you would choose to name. The inexpensive coffee houses on Yorkville Avenue have been replaced

now by expensive boutiques and sidewalk cafés. Today, instead of having to travel to Paris or Budapest, you can sit in Toronto, under an umbrella, drink some wine, and watch the world go by. The Hungarians started it all.

Kensington Market originally served Toronto's Jewish community, but today in its stores you can buy the favourite delicacies of every ethnic group. There is a carnival atmosphere as merchants cry out, "Here look at my cabbages," "Come over here, I'll give you a deal." Around the corner a free-enterpriser is selling live carp out of a kind of bathtub on wheels. Unable to speak the language? It doesn't matter, most of the bargaining is done by pointing fingers, shaking heads, and waving arms.

Left: Yorkville Avenue

Above: Kensington Market

There is a new business in Toronto that consists of buying older houses near the downtown core of the city, refurbishing them, and selling them at a profit to couples who want an alternative to the surburban lifestyle. Although there have been some problems (the poor, for instance, have been left with little alternative but to go into public housing), the effects have been mainly positive. It has revitalized the city core. When people live downtown, they care about it, and it shows. Old houses take on fresh coats of paint, the streets on summer evenings are turned over to strolling couples, families sitting on their front porches, or kids avoiding bedtime, instead of muggers and robbers.

A good example of urban renewal by private enterprise is Mirvish Village on Markham Street. Edwin Mirvish runs Honest Ed's, the world's first discount department store, at the corner of Bloor and Markham Street. Ed bought up the houses behind his store and applied to Toronto's City Council for a change in the bylaws so that he could level the houses and create a parking lot. Council wasn't too pleased with this proposal, so Ed suggested instead that he refurbish the houses and rent them out as artists' studios, restaurants and boutiques, in keeping with a village atmosphere.

Opponents of the new plan pointed out that in time the proposed village could be easily converted into the initially proposed parking lot. City Council, in its wisdom, pondered the fact that Ed had recently saved the ailing

Markham Street Village

Royal Alexandra Theatre from the wrecker's hammer. If anyone could make the new idea work it must certainly be Ed. And as to his motives, didn't he call himself "Honest" Ed?

Ed received his approval, waved his magic wand, and today there still isn't a parking lot in sight, but Mirvish Village on Markham Street is the focus of a vibrant lively community. A community that has not restricted itself only to Markham Street but has naturally spread out to all points of the compass. Mirvish Village has even

been declared, by that wise city council, a tourist attraction, thereby allowing the boutique parts of the village to join with the restaurants and conduct business on Sundays.

Other private money, taking note of Ed's success with the Village, moved in to the east and west of Markham Street along Bloor Street. Suddenly an entire section of the city has been renewed, and it did not cost a cent of the tax-payer's money. We almost lost it for fear of a small parking lot.

Right: King Street at Bay Street

Above: Roblin's Mill, Black Creek Pioneer Village

Another example of what money can do is seen at the corner of King and Bay Streets. Here are the offices of the stockbrokers, lawyers, bankers, industrialists, and promoters who control huge empires that they never see. They deal in stock certificates, bonds, treasury bills, dollars, pounds, lire, and francs. They make deals, draw up contracts, and raise money so that the nation can function.

High up in the rarified atmosphere of the fortieth floor, decisions are made in a matter of minutes that will affect the lives of millions of people. Decisions made here today might determine whether or not you have a job tomorrow. This is the stuff of power, and it seems to hang in the very air.

By contrast, Black Creek Pioneer Village in the north of Toronto takes you back to a time when things were simpler and more down-to-earth. This reconstruction of a small village of 1867 has a less frantic pace, and Roblin's Mill, with its four floors, is the tallest building in town.

A hundred miles from Toronto, just down the Queen Elizabeth Highway, is Niagara Falls, the eighth wonder of the world. Most residents of the Golden Horseshoe will tell you that they would never be caught dead gawking over the railing at the thundering waters, or dressing up in oilskins to take a wet river ride on the Maid of the Mist tour boat.

In spite of our blasé attitude towards this great spectacle, most of us do find ourselves, at least one a year acting as tour guides for out-of-province visitors. The Falls is a lot of fun. Not only can you view both the Canadian and the American Falls but you can visit a wax museum and zoo and aquarium, go up in a tower, visit a hydro dam, view the whirlpool from the cable car, tell the time on a huge floral clock, visit a greenhouse, go golfing, swimming, or picnicing. If all of this isn't enough, you can get married and spend your honeymoon here.

Once you have seen everything at the Falls, drive down the Niagara Parkway until you come to Niagara-on-the-Lake. Here is a town steeped in history, where time seems to have stood still. Originally settled by Loyalists escaping the American Revolution, Governor John Graves Simcoe declared it in 1792 the first capital of the Province of Upper Canada. Simcoe later moved his capital to Toronto, and in the War of 1812, American invaders burned Niagara-on-the-Lake to the ground. Lovingly rebuilt after the War of 1812, the town has that air of quiet dignity, mixed with a certain amount of independent

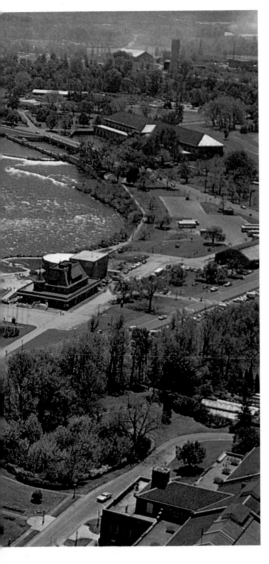

superiority that comes from having been around for a long time.

The Shaw Festival Theatre was founded at Niagara-on-the-Lake in 1962. Instead of by American troops, the town is invaded and occupied every summer by theatre lovers from the United States and Canada.

Hamilton, mid-way between Toronto and Niagara Falls, marches to the beat of heavy industry.

Left: Canadian Falls,
Niagara Falls

Above: Niagara-on-the-Lake

Below: Hamilton

Cottage Country

Cottage country occupies that land of lakes, rocks, and forest on the southern edge of the Canadian Shield. Areas such as the Bruce Peninsula, Muskoka Lakes, Lake of Bays, Kawartha Lakes, and Georgian Bay, have huge phantom populations of city dwellers. These city dwellers are in residence for part of the summer and on most weekends but spend their working days in jobs in cities like Toronto.

Modern man feels that modern society has cut him off from his primeval beginnings. The simple outdoor life, beside a wilderness lake, is his way of recapturing the cherished values of years past. The wilderness-experience idea has become so popular lately that it has become self-defeating. Some shorelines are rimmed with city-like homes every hundred feet, so that the area is closer to a city subdivision than to a wilderness.

If city dwellers are honest with themselves, they will admit that generally they are too accustomed to the gadgets and comforts of modern city life ever to be able to experience the pioneering life of their ancestors. Yet the cottage-experience and the camping trip are a partial return to the old ways, and for this reason ought to be cherished.

Those highways leading to cottage country on Friday night in the summer months are always packed tight with carloads of people seeking to escape the city heat for a couple of days. Drivers with fairy-tale visions of huge fish, cool waters, wilderness expanses, and little cabins beside lovely lakes dancing in their heads charge headlong in a mad bumper-to-bumper rush towards the north. Sporty-looking "muscle cars" packed tight with young swingers off to an exciting few days at the beach or lodge jostle with mid-sized sedans occupied by lonely summer bachelors off to spend the weekend with families staying all summer at the cottage. Wedged into this mad crowd is the recreational vehicle, summer home of that new breed of camper who has to take the city along with him. Road-hogging rigs that contain everything, including the kitchen sink, piled up with canoes and motorcycles, or towing outboard boats, groan and wheeze up the hills.

Cottager's and camper's vehicles jam the three northbound lanes of highway 400 north of Toronto, near King City, on a hot summer Friday evening.

I always make it a point to rise with the sun on a Saturday morning, no matter how heavy the traffic or how late I arrived at the cottage on Friday night. I go north to escape the telephone, work, deadlines, traffic, pollution, noise, personal problems, even some of my friends. The quiet beauty of the early morning refreshes my soul and renews my faith in life itself. It's a time of quiet contemplation, a time to unload the circuits of the mind, a time when problems seem to solve themselves.

Algonquin Park is the last stronghold of true wilderness in the area. Here travel is by canoe and distances are measured by lakes paddled or portages traversed. You have to carry everything on your back across those portages, and so, of necessity, possessions are reduced to a bare minimum. A week in Algonquin will teach one that the most important things in life are, first, a full stomach and, second, a roof over one's head. If a campsite in Algonquin is not to your liking, perhaps the friendly sands of Wasaga Beach are what

you crave. I used to spend almost every weekend at Wasaga, until I happened to meet a girl there that I later married. Wasaga used to be a triumph of free enterprise. A strip of beautiful sand beach, lined with cheap old cottages for rent, interspersed with even cheaper and older motels and lodges. This decadence was crowned with a midway and several drink-and-dance places featuring rock groups rejected by the Toronto bars. Frankly, it was a fun place for a young person on the make.

Left: Severn River

*Right: Sawyer Lake,
Algonquin Provincial Park*

Centre: Wasaga Beach

Bottom: Horseshoe Valley

The Ontario government has declared it a provincial park now and leveled most of the cheap motels and cottages, expropriated the best drinking spot on the beach, and put up all kinds of signs telling you what you can and can't do. In spite of all of this, it's still a fun place.

While the summer season attracts the biggest crowds to cottage country, more and more summer residents are winterizing their cottages and heading north to skate, ski, and snowmobile.

With the changing of the leaves and the first snows of winter, cottage country takes on a more relaxed air. Locals who put in sixteen hour days all summer, catering to city slickers, have a chance to close up shop and go fishing. The woods are beautiful at this time of year. Trails are uncrowded and free of annoying blackflies and mosquitoes. Towns such as Tobermory, Parry Sound, Gravenhurst, Minden, Bancroft, and Barry's Bay shed their summer carnival atmosphere and become sleepy little communities again, where residents have the time to stop and chat about their grandchildren or the playoff possibilities of the local hockey team.

I shared a campfire once with a couple of citizens of Huntsville I met in the fall wilderness of Algonquin Park. They worked hard all summer long in businesses associated with the tourist trade, and spent the rest of the year enjoying themselves. Their terse comment about their nine-month holiday was: "Muskoka beats working."

Small Town Ontario

The small towns of central Ontario preserve the old Ontario that has largely disappeared from our big cities. Conservative in politics and religion, wary of strangers, and resolutely independent, these towns are not quick to adopt the latest fad from the outside world.

It's true that there may be a McDonald's, a new shopping centre, or a subdivision on the outskirts of town, but it seems these interlopers are afraid to violate the inner sanctum of main street. This is where the feed store, the catalogue-order office, the beverage room of the Empire Hotel, and the restaurant specializing in Chinese and Canadian food reign supreme. Farmers, in their bib overalls, still congregate on Saturday mornings at the corner. Their wives do the shopping while they talk about milk production and their kids ride their bikes without fear of being run over.

The church is the social centre of these towns, and the Orange Lodge, while it isn't as strong as it used to be, still commands respect. Everyone knows you in a small town so you are a somebody, not because you may be a big business man or a television star, but just because you are there.

Below: Port Perry, Right: Orangeville

The area around the twin cities of Kitchener and Waterloo has a large community of Mennonites. Deeply religious, these land-loving farmers reject the values and machinery of modern society. Their insistence on using the horse and buggy has made them the best judges of horseflesh in the province. Waterloo county is one of the few places where buggy wheels and harnesses are readily available. Roads are made extra wide to accommodate both horses and cars, and road signs warn motorists to be on the lookout for buggies.

Small towns tend to adapt themselves to the changing seasons. When winter snows cover the ground you will hear the roar of the snowmobile or the slap of a hockey puck bouncing against the boards of the town's arena. Spring finds kids catching suckers in nearby ponds, while the adults engage in such end of winter foolishness as bathtub races down local rivers. Summer is a time for the old swimming hole, tending your prize rose bushes, spending warm summer evenings cooking over a barbecue, and getting to know children who do not have to go to school the next day. The red leaves of autumn, the football games at the high school, the fall fair, and the new friends made at school, complete the cycle of the seasons. In small towns, as sure as spring will follow winter, life will always be the same. A bit of permanence in a rapidly changing world.

Stephen Leacock poked fun at small-town Ontario in his many books of short stories. His works were immensely popular when they were published. All of Canada laughed at the antics of the inhabitants of his imaginary town of Mariposa. When the good citizens of Orillia learned that the mythical Mariposa was in fact Orillia; that they were the butt of Leacock's wit, and that Leacock was spending his summers observing and writing in that big place on Brewery Bay just outside of town, they were not amused. If Leacock had lived in the American west, instead of in conservative Ontario, I am sure the author would have been lynched and his house burned to the ground. As it turned out, Leacock lived to a ripe old age, and the home is still standing and set aside as a museum.

Orillia is no longer the Mariposa that Leacock wrote about. But the townspeople now delight in his memory and even hold a summer festival of the arts – called, of course, the Mariposa Festival – in his honour.

Left: Near St. Jacobs

Above: Leacock House, Orillia

Below: Bus Stop, Orillia

*Right: Sulky Race,
Lindsay Fall Fair*

People will still strike up a conversation at the bus stop in Orillia. But if you really want to see central Ontario with its hair down, visit one of the province's fall fairs. Rural people raise livestock, grow prize vegetables, and all year round work out recipes for jam or pie in anticipation of winning a blue ribbon at the October fair. The hot, work-filled days of summer are over, the harvest is in and sold, pockets jingle with crop money, there is a touch of frost and a ring of excitement in the air. It's time to have some fun.

Valley Country

Eastern Ontario is the oldest, most historic part of the province. Champlain passed through in 1613, looking for a route to the Indies. Kingston was founded by French fur traders in 1673. The United Empire Loyalists and Scottish Highlanders took up land along the valleys of the Saint Lawrence, Rideau, and Ottawa rivers after the American Revolution.

Lumbering was, at one time, a major industry in the valleys. The huge white pine and the timber rafts are gone now, as are the lumberjacks and the sawmills. The Rideau Canal connecting Kingston and Ottawa was a busy commercial artery, but nowadays with railways and improved highways the canal only carries pleasure craft.

Ottawa, Cornwall, Brockville, and Kingston are prosperous cities, but they are not typical of the Valley. Ottawa owes its prosperity to its position as the nation's capital, and the others to their location on the St. Lawrence Seaway.

If you travel inland, away from the St. Lawrence and Ottawa rivers to such long-established towns such as Perth, Smith's Falls, Kemptville, Renfrew, and Eganville, you will find empty houses and abandoned factories. It is obvious that they have seen busier, more prosperous days.

You can visit the Ottawa area in any season, and there is always something to see and do. In winter the frozen Rideau Canal is turned into the world's longest skating rink. In summer you can watch the colourful Changing of the Guard, as they march back and forth in front of the Parliament Buildings in their red uniforms and black bearskin hats. Spring brings the tulip display, and the fall the beautiful red and yellow leaves of the Gatineau hills.

Government being the main industry of the city, the Parliament Buildings dominate everything from their lofty perch on top of Parliament Hill. Here men gather from all parts of the country to make decisions, or to try to influence decisions, that affect the lives of each and every Canadian. As befits a national capital, Ottawa has been made a showplace. The National Gallery, the National Museum, the National Arts Centre, the National Library and Public Archives, and the National Film Board Gallery, to name but a few of the city's attractions, are all worth a visit at any time of year.

Lunch hour skaters brave the cold of an Ottawa winter day, to glide over the frozen Rideau Canal within sight of Canada's Parliament Buildings.

Top: Changing of the Guard,
Parliament Buildings, Ottawa

Right: St. Lawrence River and a Few
of the Thousand Islands at Ivy Lea

Middle: Kingston

Bottom: Hitching a stagecoach
behind Cook's Tavern
Upper Canada Village, Morrisburg

On summer mornings eager tourists gather on the front lawn of Canada's Parliament Buildings in Ottawa to view the colourful ceremony of the Changing of the Guard. Sharp on the stroke of 10:00 a.m. the Old and New Guards divisions, accompanied by a Colour Party and two military marching bands, step smartly on the field. The forty-five minute ceremony is a grand display of tradition, pageantry, and precision marching to stirring military music, by the red-coated Guards.

Kingston was established in 1673 by the French fur trader De La Salle. Fort Henry was constructed in 1813 and the city became the provincial capital for a short time in the early 1840's.

Today, with its military base, university, military college, and penitentiary system, Kingston is a busy bustling place. It has been able to retain its sense of history as well, and the morning sun still shines on the domes of those buildings constructed so many years ago when the city was the capital of Upper Canada.

Upper Canada Village is an example of another kind of historical preservation. During the construction of the St. Lawrence Seaway in the 1950's, it became obvious to the Government of Ontario that many of the province's historic buildings would disappear beneath the waters of the new Seaway. These buildings were moved to a new site, and a complete village, operating as it might have one hundred years ago, was created near Morrisburg.

Step through the toll gate at the village entrance and you step back in time. A stage coach is being hitched up behind Cook's Tavern; women are spinning wool in the McDiarmid house; the huge up-and-down blade is biting into a giant log in the water-powered sawmill; a boat full of passengers is arriving at the village dock; the blacksmith is talking to a frightened horse he is trying to shoe; and the smell of new-baked bread combined with the dry heat of the baker's oven tingles in your nostrils as you walk past the bakery. This is not the dull stuff of museum showcases. This is the living history of eastern Ontario, and you are there.

The Thousand Islands area of the St. Lawrence extends from the river's start at Kingston to a point fifty miles downstream. The name is not an accurate one, as there are, in fact, 1,870 islands. A recreational area for many years, most of the islands in private hands are studded with summer homes. The remainder have been turned into public parks. Majestic cruisers and canoes alike thread the narrow channels of the archipelago.

Bill Brooks

Born and raised near Toronto, Bill Brooks has been conducting a love affair with his home province of Ontario as long as he can remember. After graduating in Economics from the University of Toronto in 1962, he worked as a photo editor and photographer. These activities carried him into every region of Canada, but he always returned to his home base, Toronto.

In 1972, wanting to become more directly involved in the creation of fine illustrated books, he struck out on his own to photograph and write. His photos for use in magazines, calendars and books have been sold worldwide to clients as diverse as National Geographic and Playgirl, to name but two. Other books illustrated or written by Bill Brooks are: Canada in Colour (1972), Ottawa: A Portrait of the Nation's Capital (1973), The Mill (1976), and Wildlife of Canada (1976).

Text and Photographs: Bill Brooks

Design: V. John Lee

Editor: John Robert Colombo

Publisher: Anthony Hawke

Printed in Canada by Heritage Press

Copyright© 1977 by Bill Brooks

All Rights Reserved.

ISBN 0-88882-007-0

Hounslow Press
A Division of Anthony R. Hawke Limited
124 Parkview Avenue
Willowdale, Ontario, Canada

M2N 3Y5